NASHVILLE PUBLIC LIBRARY
FOUNDATION

*This book given
to the Nashville Public Library
through the generosity of the*
**Dollar General
Literacy Foundation**

NPLF.ORG

Women in the Environmental Sciences

Major Women in Science

MAJOR WOMEN IN SCIENCE

Women in the Environmental Sciences

Shaina Indovino

Mason Crest

Mason Crest
450 Parkway Drive, Suite D
Broomall, Pennsylvania 19008
www.masoncrest.com

Printed and bound in the United States of America.

First printing
9 8 7 6 5 4 3 2 1

Series ISBN: 978-1-4222-2923-1
ISBN: 978-1-4222-2927-9
ebook ISBN: 978-1-4222-8896-2

The Library of Congress has cataloged the
        hardcopy format(s) as follows:

        Library of Congress Cataloging-in-Publication Data

Indovino, Shaina Carmel.
  Women in the environmental sciences / Shaina Indovino.
      pages cm. -- (Major women in science)
  Audience: Grade 7 to 8.
  Includes bibliographical references and index.
  ISBN 978-1-4222-2927-9 (hardcover) -- ISBN 978-1-4222-2923-1 (series) -- ISBN 978-1-4222-8896-2 (ebook)
  1. Environmental sciences--Biography--Juvenile literature. 2. Women scientists--Biography--Juvenile literature. 3. Women environmentalists--Biography--Juvenile literature. 4. Environmental sciences--Vocational guidance--Juvenile literature. I. Title.
  GE55.I54 2014
  363.7092'52--dc23
                              2013011150

Produced by Vestal Creative Services.
www.vestalcreative.com

Contents

Introduction

Have you wondered about how the natural world works? Are you curious about how science could help sick people get better? Do you want to learn more about our planet and universe? Are you excited to use technology to learn and share ideas? Do you want to build something new?

Scientists, engineers, and doctors are among the many types of people who think deeply about science and nature, who often have new ideas on how to improve life in our world.

We live in a remarkable time in human history. The level of understanding and rate of progress in science and technology have never been greater. Major advances in these areas include the following:

- Computer scientists and engineers are building mobile and Internet technology to help people access and share information at incredible speeds.
- Biologists and chemists are creating medicines that can target and get rid of harmful cancer cells in the body.
- Engineers are guiding robots on Mars to explore the history of water on that planet.
- Physicists are using math and experiments to estimate the age of the universe to be greater than 13 billion years old.
- Scientists and engineers are building hybrid cars that can be better for our environment.

Scientists are interested in discovering and understanding key principles in nature, including biological, chemical, mathematical, and physical aspects of our world. Scientists observe, measure, and experiment in a systematic way in order to test and improve their understanding. Engineers focus on applying scientific knowledge and math to find creative solutions for technical problems and to develop real products for people to use. There are many types of engineering, including computer, electrical, mechanical, civil, chemical, and biomedical engineering. Some people have also found that studying science or engineering can help them succeed in other professions such as law, business, and medicine.

Both women and men can be successful in science and engineering. This book series highlights women leaders who have made significant contributions across many scientific fields, including chemistry, medicine, anthropology, engineering, and physics. Historically, women have faced barriers to training and building careers in science,

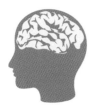

which makes some of these stories even more amazing. While not all barriers have been overcome, our society has made tremendous progress in educating and advancing women in science. Today, there are schools, organizations, and resources to enable women to pursue careers as scientists or engineers at the highest levels of achievement and leadership.

The goals of this series are to help you:

1. Learn about women scientists, engineers, doctors, and inventors who have made a major impact in science and our society
2. Understand different types of science and engineering
3. Explore science and math in school and real life

You can do a lot of things to learn more about science, math, and engineering. Explore topics in books or online, take a class at school, go to science camp, or do experiments at home. More important, talk to a real scientist! Call or e-mail your local college to find students and professors. They would love to meet with you. Ask your doctors about their education and training. Or you can check out these helpful resources:

- *Nova* has very cool videos about science, including profiles on real-life women scientists and engineers: www.pbs.org/wgbh/nova.
- *National Geographic* has excellent photos and stories to inspire people to care about the planet: science.nationalgeographic.com/science.
- Here are examples of online courses for students, of which many are free to use:
    1. Massachusetts Institute of Technology (MIT) OpenCourseWare highlights for high school: ocw.mit.edu/high-school.
    2. Khan Academy tutorials and courses: www.khanacademy.org.
    3. Stanford University Online, featuring video courses and programs for middle and high school students: online.stanford.edu.

Other skills will become important as you get older. Build strong communication skills, such as asking questions and sharing your ideas in class. Ask for advice or help when needed from your teachers, mentors, tutors, or classmates. Be curious and resilient: learn from your successes and mistakes. The best scientists do.

Learning science and math is one of the most important things that you can do in school. Knowledge and experience in these areas will teach you how to think and how the world works and can provide you with many adventures and paths in life. I hope you will explore science—you could make a difference in this world.

Ann Lee-Karlon, PhD
President
Association for Women in Science
San Francisco, California

1

What Does It Take to Be an Environmental Scientist?

Have you ever looked at nature and wondered why things are the way there are? Why does it rain more near a lake than on dry land? What does the ozone layer have to do with the temperature of the Earth? How does a new housing development affect the animals and plants that already lived on that land? Environmental scientists observe nature. They investigate relationships between different elements of the environment. They find answers to questions like these.

The environment is very **complex**. Water, rocks, sunlight, and soil all interact with one another, creating a place where living things can grow. The climate is influenced by the **intensity** and angle of the Sun as it strikes the Earth. Weather patterns are shaped by the way air rises and moves in the atmosphere. Climate and weather create unique patterns of heat and moisture, which in turn create the conditions where certain life forms can thrive. **Nutrients** in the soil allow plants to grow. Animals eat those plants, and eventually die. Decomposers, such as mushrooms, worms, or bacteria, break down dead organisms, so that they return to the soil, adding to the nutrients. Everything in nature is connected within the cycles of life.

Because of this, a problem in a particular **ecosystem** can have any number of different explanations. An environmental scientist has to carefully sort through the various factors, determining how they interact. Finding solutions to an environmental problem is not an easy job—but these scientists are passionate about protecting our planet.

Why Be an Environmental Scientist?

Environmental scientists around the world work together to make sure the Earth will be here for future generations. As more and more people become aware of the problems of pollution and climate change, governments, industries, and communities are looking for ways to solve these problems. Meanwhile, the human population is continuing to grow, and more parts of the world are using technology that contributes to these problems.

The interaction between the natural world and human populations is complicated. Developing nations feel they should have the right to build industries that contribute to their economies—even though they may also contribute to pollution and other environmental problems. People may be worried more about getting a job at a new factory in their community than about the pollution that the factory may cause in their environment.

Environmental scientists study these problems. They try to find solutions that ʻ ʻ be good for humans while protecting the planet on which we live. They give

An environmental science student takes a water sample, which she will bring back to the lab to study further.

advice on how to fix existing problems, as well as how to prevent ones that haven't happened yet.

Education

Environmental science involves a lot of different fields. These include biology, earth science, chemistry, ecology, and physics. The environment can be studied from many angles, from the most basic chemical composition of soil and water, to the various life forms that inhabit it, to the history of the rocks and hills. All these things interact as well, so most environmental scientists have a wide scientific background that will allow them to have a grasp of the big picture.

Right now, if you think you might be interested in this field, you can start out by simply paying attention to the natural world. Notice the different species of plants and animals that live in your region. Pay attention to weather patterns. Study rocks. Read books, watch nature shows on TV, and check out websites. Visit a nature preserve or park and talk to the people who work there. Find out if you could volunteer to help in any environmental projects.

To further your knowledge, you will need to go to college. **Entry-level** environmental science jobs require at least a bachelor's degree in environmental science or another natural science, such as biology, chemistry, or **geosciences**. If you want to get promotions, you may need to go on to get a master's degree. A

Part of an environmental scientist's job may be to educate others. Here, the environmental director for Naval Facilities Engineering Command is explaining to high school student about electric vehicles and other environmentally friendly means of transportation used by the Navy.

doctoral degree is typically needed for some advanced research positions or if you want to teach environmental sciences in a college or university.

If you get a bachelor's degree in environmental science you'll usually get a broad background in the natural sciences. Students typically take courses in biology, chemistry, geology, and physics. You may also take specialized courses in **hydrology**, **waste management**, and **fluid mechanics**, as well as classes in **environmental policy** and regulation.

While you're in college, look for opportunities to work with **computer modeling**, **data analysis**, and **geographic information systems** through classes and **internships**. If you have experience in these programs you'll be better prepared to compete for jobs out in the work world.

Character

Environmental scientists need to be **passionate** about what they do. If you believe strongly in what you're doing, you'll have the energy and commitment to work hard in your field, year after year.

Like all scientists, environmental scientists need good analytical skills. This means they can carefully study information. They can break it down into pieces and draw conclusions from it. They must consider all possible methods and solutions in their analyses.

Environmental scientists also need interpersonal skills. They typically work on teams with scientists, engineers, and technicians, so they need to be able to work well with others.

They also need problem-solving skills. Environmental scientists try to find the best possible solution to problems that affect the environment. They need to be able to think outside the box, considering new ideas that no one else has come up with yet.

In addition, environmental scientists must be able to communicate clearly. This means they must have good speaking and writing skills. They often give presentations that explain their findings, and they need to convince others to accept their recommendations. They also write technical reports that explain their methods, findings, and recommendations.

New technology is helping to expanding the field of environmental science. This is one of NASA's high-altitude earth science aircraft used for atmospheric sampling.

Environmental science is a relatively new field, but it has a growing importance in our world today. Back in the twentieth century, when this scientific field was just getting started, courageous and intelligent women were some of the scientists who helped to build its foundations.

Words to Know

Complex: intricate, complicated.
Intensity: how strong something is.
Nutrients: substances living things need to function, but cannot make themselves.

Ecosystem: a biological community of living things and the environment they live in.

Entry-level: the most basic; requiring the least amount of experience.

Geosciences: the study of the earth's structure and the processes that shape it.

Hydrology: the science of water.

Waste management: the way in which waste (including feces, urine, and garbage) is collected, disposed of, and cleaned.

Fluid mechanics: the study of how liquids and gases move.

Environmental policy: a course of action a government creates to manage how humans use the natural world.

Computer modeling: using a computer program to predict the results of a process.

Data analysis: the process of looking at and making conclusions about pieces of information.

Geographic information systems: a computer technology that collects and analyzes knowledge about the physical features of the earth's surface.

Internships: temporary training programs for students studying how to do a particular job.

Passionate: having strong feelings about something.

Find Out More

Bio Careers, "Getting Started with Environmental Sciences"
www.biocareers.com/resource/getting-started-environmental-sciences

Breton, Mary Joy. *Women Pioneers: For the Environment*. Boston: Northeastern University Press, 2000.

Christensen, Norman L. *The Environment and You*. Boston: Benjamin Cummings, 2013.

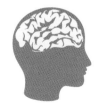

Rachel Carson:
The Woman Who Warned the World About Pesticides

2

Rachel Carson woke the world up to a very real danger. Her life proves that if you are **persistent** enough, you can truly make a difference!

Rachel Carson was born on May 27, 1907, and she grew up in a rural area of Pennsylvania. As a young girl, she enjoyed reading, writing, and exploring the world outside. One of her favorite subjects to read about was the ocean and the life within it.

When Rachel went away to college, she majored in biology. She graduated from the Pennsylvania College for Women in 1929.

Not that many women graduated from college during the 1920s. Going on to graduate school was even less expected of a woman, but Rachel wanted to continue her education. She went on to study and work at John Hopkins University. She earned a master's degree in **zoology**.

After leaving school, Rachel began working for the U.S. Bureau of Fisheries. She used her knowledge of science to write about nature, especially water habitats. She wrote for a radio show that was intended to get people interested in nature, and she also wrote articles about the natural world for magazines. In 1936, she became the editor in chief of all publications for the Bureau of Fisheries. In her role at the Bureau of Fisheries, she continued to write—this time writing pamphlets about how to reduce our impact on the Earth.

The ocean had always fascinated Rachel, and now, as a part of her professional role, she had the chance to study it. In 1952, she published one of her studies, *The Sea Around Us*. The book described the ocean and how it is changing.

Rachel's writing about her studies became so popular that she decided to dedicate her life completely to her own work. She resigned from her government job and began studying nature and writing full time, using her skills to spread knowledge about the natural world.

Some of her writings were meant to get others interested in nature, including young people. She believed strongly that humans needed to understand that they are part of nature. What makes us different from the other parts of nature is how much of an effect we have on it. Humans can cause a lot of harm to the natural world.

Rachel became more and more concerned with pesticides' affect on nature. After World War II, the use of pesticides within the United States had risen. Pesticides, chemicals designed to kill any type of pest, were meant to protect crops—but humans didn't realize that they also hurt other animals and disrupted the balance of an ecosystem. Rachel became very aware of how serious these dangers were. She decided to devote herself to making the public aware as well. In 1962, she released her findings in a book titled *Silent Spring*. The book described the terrible effects pesticides were having on wildlife and the entire environment.

Silent Spring became a bestseller. As a result, so many people other people became worried about pesticides that the government started doing its own

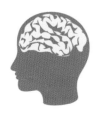

Like most environmental scientists, Rachel had to be willing to get her feet wet! Here she is taking water samples, so that she can study the effects of pesticides on marine life.

research as well. Eventually, the chemicals in pesticides were regulated and restricted. Many chemical companies viewed Rachel as their enemy, however. The chemical companies tried to prove her findings wrong because they were bad for business. Today, however, many people still read her book. Rachel changed the world.

In 1964, just two years after the publication of *Silent Spring*, Rachel died. She will always be remembered, though. She helped set the standards for environmental science. Even after her death, Rachel continued to receive honors for her contributions to science, including the Presidential Medal of Freedom, which was given to her in 1980, sixteen years after her death.

Rachel Carson 19

Words to Know

Persistent: never giving up.
Zoology: the study of animals.

Find Out More

Carson, Rachel. *Silent Spring*. Boston: Houghton Mifflin, 2002.

Carson, Rachel, and Nick Kelsh. *The Sense of Wonder*. New York: HarperCollins, 1998.

Kudlinski, Kathleen V., and Ted Lewin. *Rachel Carson: Pioneer of Ecology*. New York, N.Y.: Puffin, 2009.

Rachel Carson, "The Life and Legacy of Rachel Carson"
www.rachelcarson.org

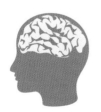

Joan Berkowitz:
Fighting Air Pollution

J oan Berkowitz started her career as a chemist. During her studies, however, she realized how chemicals were harming the environment. From then
on, she devoted her life to protecting the natural world. She helped others
understand what causes pollution and how it affects the environment.

Joan was born in New York in 1931. As a young girl, she loved science and
was very good at it. Joan's mother was a supporter of women's equality, and her
mother's conviction fueled Joan's determination to become a scientist. One of
Joan's earliest teachers was positive Joan would become a scientist one day—
and Joan would one day prove her right.

In 1952, she graduated with a bachelor's degree in chemistry. She wanted to
go on to Princeton University, but at that time, women were not allowed to earn

...emistry graduate degrees at Princeton. Instead, Joan attended the University of Illinois, which allowed women into its graduate program.

After earning her PhD, Joan began working in 1957. She joined the consulting firm of Arthur D. Little two years later. One of her earliest jobs there was researching materials that could be used in a spacecraft. The conditions in both outer space and the Earth's atmosphere required materials that could withstand extreme heat, cold, and pressure. Joan discovered that one material worked better than others: molybdenum disilicide. This was only one of many breakthroughs for Joan. She also worked with a material that is now used in solar panels.

Early computer technology was developing during this time, and Joan was one of the first scientists to use computers to predict how materials would react to certain conditions. This was important, because field tests could be expensive and dangerous. By using computer **simulations**, scientists could have a better idea of what might happen before actual materials are wasted.

Joan Berkowitz's knowledge about chemicals and the way they interact with the environment eventually led to her interest in waste management. She realized that the way we dispose of hazardous waste could be done better. Her suggestions were published in several places, including the Environmental Protection Agency's First Report to Congress on Hazardous Waste. She also investigated how we can reduce the amount of pollution created by burning coal. Her work led to new alternatives to coal power.

Joan's success as a respected scientist led to new opportunities. In the 1980s, she became a vice president and later head of the Environmental Business World

Waste Management

The human population is growing, and so is the amount of waste we produce. Some of this waste is hazardous. This means it can hurt the environment and wildlife. As technology improves, the amount of hazardous waste we create is also increasing. Joan developed new alternatives for managing waste, which are still used today.

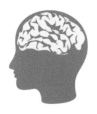

Joan in her laboratory in 1973. One of the things she has worked on is a technique called "scrubbing" to remove sulfur dioxide—which can cause acid rain when it enters the atmosphere—from coal exhaust, using a chemical reaction.

Wide section of Arthur D. Little. She made history in 1979 when she became the first female president of the Electrochemical Society. Joan has also served as a professor teaching about environmental management. In addition to her dedication to the environment, Joan cares about women's issues. She is a role model for young women who love science and nature.

Words to Know
Simulations: imitations, reproductions, models.

Find Out More
Chemical Heritage Foundation, "Joan Berkowitz"
www.chemheritage.org/discover/online-resources/chemistry-in-history/
themes/public-and-environmental-health/environmental-chemistry/berkowitz.aspx

Chemistry at Illinois, "Sylvia M. Stoesser Lecturer 2002-03—Joan B. Berkowitz"
www.chemistry.illinois.edu/events/lectures/SM_Stoesser_Lectures_in_
Chemistry/Joan_Berkowitz.html

McNeill, J. R. *Something New Under the Sun: An Environmental History of the Twentieth-Century World*. New York: Norton, 2001.

Wangari Maathai: Nobel Prize Winner

Wangari Maathai was a strong-willed woman. Throughout her life, she tried to make the world better in several ways. One way was by being an environmental scientist. She was also a politician. She worked hard for her women, for her nation, and for the planet.

Wangari was born on April 1, 1940 in Kenya. Even at a young age, education was important to her. She attended the only Catholic high school for girls in the entire country. When it was time to go to college, she was given the opportunity to study in the United States. Wangari packed up her things and moved across the globe to Kansas where she attended the Mount St. Scholastica College.

Out of all of the subjects she studied there, Wangari liked science the most. She majored in biology and minored in chemistry and German. Then she went

These women are working to both improve the Earth and their own lives. Wangari's Green Belt Movement reduced poverty among women and at the same time helped protect Kenya's environment.

on to pursue a master's degree in biology at the University of Pittsburgh. While she was there, she first became interested in environmental protection. The air pollution of the city was an enormous problem at the time, and environmentalists were speaking out about it.

After earning her master's degree, Wangari then spent time studying in Germany and Kenya. In 1971, she became the first woman in Eastern and Central Africa to receive a PhD. Her PhD was in **anatomy**.

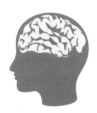

Wangari wasted no time getting to work. In 1976, she became chairperson of the Department of Veterinary Anatomy, the first woman to hold this position in Kenya.

One of the first problems she attacked had to do with **deforestation**. The world was drastically changing because so many trees are being cut down. Other plants and animals depend on trees for their habitats. The Earth needs the oxygen that trees produce. Wangari tried to reverse the damage done by deforestation by getting communities to plant more trees together.

Human rights was another important issue for Wangari. She believed all people should be treated equally, no matter what their race, religion, or gender was. As a female who had to struggle to obtain an education, she knew what it was like to face discrimination—and now she wanted to help others. She became the chairman of the National Council of Women in Kenya.

Wangari understood that the fate of the planet is intertwined with human life. What is good for the Earth will ultimately be good for human communities—and what damages the Earth will also damage human communities. Human rights and environmental issues are connected.

In 1977, Wangari, with the help of the National Council of Women, founded the Green Belt Movement, which helped women and the environment at the same time. Many women in Kenya were having a hard time finding food, water, and firewood. The Green Belt Movement gave these women help and advice. It worked to reduce poverty and promote conservation.

In 2003, Wangari joined the Kenyan Parliament. She was the assistant minister for Environment and Natural Resources. Her advice helped the government make decisions about what to do in situations that would affect the environment.

Wangari became famous around the world for her struggle for democracy, human rights, and environmental conservation. She addressed the United Nations on a number of occasions and spoke on behalf of women at special sessions of the General Assembly during the five-year review of the Earth Summit. In 2004, she was awarded the Nobel Peace Prize for her work. She was the first African woman to receive this honor.

In 2005, she was appointed Goodwill Ambassador to the Congo Basin Forest Ecosystem, and in 2007, she was invited to be co-chair of the Congo Basin

Wangari Maathai 27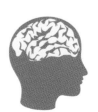

Earth Summit

In 1992, 172 governments participated in a special UN conference on the environment. The issues addressed included:

- toxic elements in gasoline, such as lead
- radioactive and other poisonous wastes
- the growing scarcity of water

Proposals were made for:

- alternative sources of energy to replace the use of fossil fuels that are linked to global climate change
- new reliance on public transportation systems in order to reduce vehicle emissions, congestion in cities, and the health problems caused by polluted air and smoke.

Fund, an initiative by the British and the Norwegian governments to help protect the Congo forests. In recognition of her deep commitment to the environment, the UN Secretary-General named Wangari a UN Messenger of Peace in December 2009, with a focus on the environment and climate change. In 2010, she became a trustee of the Karura Forest Environmental Education Trust, which was established to safeguard the public land for whose protection she had fought for almost twenty years. That same year, in partnership with the University of Nairobi, she founded the Wangari Maathai Institute for Peace and Environmental Studies (WMI). The WMI will bring together academic research—in land use, forestry, agriculture, resource-based conflicts, and peace studies—with the Green Belt Movement approach.

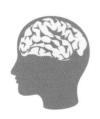

Wangari Maathai planting trees in Kenya with a new generation.

In 2009, the UN Secretary-General inducted Wangari as a UN Messenger of Peace. Wangari said, "We are called to assist the Earth to heal her wounds and in the process heal our own—indeed to embrace the whole of creation in all its diversity, beauty and wonder. Recognizing that sustainable development, democracy and peace are indivisible is an idea whose time has come."

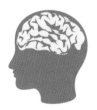

The Nobel Peace Prize

The Nobel Peace Prize is one of the most important prizes a person can receive. Since 1901, it has been awarded each year (with some exceptions) to those who have "done the most or the best work for fraternity between nations, for the abolition or reduction of standing armies and for the holding and promotion of peace congresses." All Nobel Peace Prize winners have done something to make the world a better, more peaceful place.

Wangari Maathai died in September of 2011, but she had accomplished a great deal in her lifetime. The organization she started, the Green Belt Movement, is still going strong. Her life is an example to everyone, proving that great passion can accomplish amazing things.

Words to Know

Anatomy: the study of the physical structure of living things.
Deforestation: the process by which all the trees in an area are cut down.

Find Out More

The Green Belt Movement
www.greenbeltmovement.org

Maathai, Wangari. *The Green Belt Movement: Sharing the Approach and the Experience.* New York: Lantern, 2003.

Maathai, Wangari. *Unbowed: A Memoir*. New York: Anchor, 2007.

Maathai, Wangari. *The Challenge for Africa*. New York: Anchor, 2010.

Elvia Niebla:
Soil Scientist

5

Some people have a drive to help others. This is certainly the case with Elvia Niebla. Not only is she a well-known soil scientist, but she has also helped people in other ways.

Elvia was born in 1945 in Arizona. As a young girl, she had an appreciation for both the outdoors and for helping others. At school, she excelled in mathematics and science.

As a Hispanic woman in the 1960s, Elvia had few career options. Educated Hispanic women were expected to be secretaries or teachers. They were not encouraged to become scientists! But Elvia knew what she wanted. She wanted to study math and science!

How Math Helps Environmental Scientists

In addition to science, Elvia was also always interested in mathematics. Math helps environmental scientists make predictions. If a certain amount of sludge is exposed to soil, for example, math equations tell scientists how far it can possibly travel. This is how Elvia and other environmental scientists can predict which organisms and human communities it might affect.

Against the odds, she did just that. In 1967, she received a bachelor's degree in zoology and chemistry from the University of Arizona. After college, she became a special education teacher. She taught mathematics and science to high school students with learning disabilities. After three years, in 1979, Elvia returned to the University of Arizona to study soil chemistry.

Soil scientists study the chemicals in soil. They examine the various things that create soil. They learn to decipher clues about the past from soil.

One of Elvia's first jobs as a soil scientist was at an archaeological center. The traditional **adobe** structures were deteriorating over time, and she was asked to help fix them. Using her knowledge of soil, she figured out exactly what the buildings were made from. Then the buildings could be restored using the same soil that was used to make them.

Five years after receiving her PhD, Elvia joined the U.S. Environmental Protection Agency (EPA). This organization tries to preserve the environment by restricting the damage humans do to it. As a soil scientist, Elvia was asked to study how sludge affects soil and the plants that grow on it. Sludge is the liquid waste that is leftover when garbage has rotted, or decomposed. It can easily seep into soil and harm the agriculture that grows in the area.

Elvia discovered that sludge can be damaging to everything in an ecosystem, not just the soil. If the sludge contaminates the soil, plants can absorb it. If animals eat those plants, they can also be exposed to toxins. If humans consume the plants or animals, they too will be harmed. This may seem like common knowledge now, but it wasn't when Elvia first did her research. It's because of

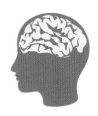

people like her that we have a better understanding of how chemicals affect the ecosystem. For her efforts, the EPA awarded her the Bronze Medal.

Since 1989, Elvia has worked as National Coordinator of the Global Change Research Program (geochange.er.usgs.gov), studying the changing global climate and its effects on trees, animals, and forests. Her job is to translate and provide scientific information to help politicians develop regulations and decide where funding should go.

Elvia says, "One year, I decided how to distribute 25 million dollars to scientists and the science projects they proposed. When the results of the environmental research are given to me, I use them to help advise politicians making the rules for the use of land. I also represent the United States at international environmental conferences and committees."

Elvia tells young women: "My advice is that you should pursue your interests no matter what they are. Don't be dissuaded by the obstacles and disbelievers that you will encounter. If you are dedicated to your dreams, you will always find a way to accomplish them."

Words to Know

Adobe: a kind of clay used for building.

Find Out More

Ditchfield, Christin. *Soil*. New York: Children's Press, 2003.

The My Hero Project, "Dr. Elvia Niebla: Soil Scientist"
www.myhero.com/go/hero.asp?hero=elvia_niebla_06

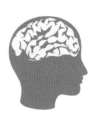

6

Susan Solomon:
Protecting the Atmosphere

The ozone layer is a very thin layer of gas that protects the surface of the Earth from the harmful rays of the sun. Recently, scientists have discovered a hole in the ozone layer. The hole allows more rays of the sun through, which is one cause of **global warming**. For a long time, scientists could not figure out what was causing the hole in the atmosphere. Finally, a group of scientists came up with a suggestion. Susan Solomon was one of those scientists.

The Atmosphere

The atmosphere is not just the oxygen we breathe. It is also composed of all the gases found on the Earth. The atmosphere also spreads far out into space around our planet. The altitude we reach when we fly in an airplane is only a fraction of how far the atmosphere extends.

Susan was born in 1956. She was interested in science even when she was young, and in high school, she entered the national science fair with a project that measured the amount of oxygen in a gas mixture. After high school, she went to Illinois Institute of Technology (IIT) and studied chemistry. From there, she went to the University of California at Berkeley. Her area of study was more **specialized** here, and she became an expert in atmospheric chemistry. Atmospheric chemists study the chemicals in the atmosphere.

After earning her PhD, Susan joined the National Oceanic and Atmospheric Administration (NOAA). Susan was the leader of a NOAA expedition that went to Antarctica in 1986 to investigate the hole in the ozone layer. They discovered one of the causes of the hole in the ozone layer—chlorofluorocarbons, or CFCs, also known as Freon. This chemical compound was being released into the atmosphere from aerosol cans and refrigerants.

Susan's discovery gained her a lot of respect. She continued to work for NOAA and became the head of the Chemistry and Climate Process Group. Today, Susan is recognized to be an expert worldwide in atmospheric science.

She has received many honors for her contributions to science. In 1994, an Antarctic glacier was named after her. Five years later, she was awarded the National Medal of Science. In 2007, she received the Nobel Peace Prize as co-chair of the Intergovernmental Panel on Climate Change for the panel's efforts

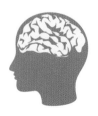

thermosphere	
80km	
	(mesopause)
mesosphere	
50km	
	(stratopause)
stratosphere	
15km	
troposphere	(tropopause)

This chart shows the layers of the atmosphere. The highest layer, the thermosphere, extends more than 80 kilometers into space around the Earth.

to protect the environment. In 2011, Susan left NOAA and began teaching at the Massachusetts Institute of Technology (MIT). As a professor of atmospheric chemistry and climate science, she continues to protect the world and make a difference by inspiring young adults to carry on her work.

Words to Know

Global warming: the process by which the earth's climate is getting hotter, caused by human activities that release carbon dioxide and other heat-trapping gases into the air.

Specialized: requiring detailed and specific knowledge and skills.

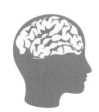

The Fate of the Ozone Layer

The discoveries made by the NOAA were taken very seriously. By 2009, every country within the United Nations agreed to restrict the use of chlorofluorocarbons. Unfortunately, this did not completely fix the problem. The CFCs already released into the atmosphere will continue to damage the ozone layer over time. The good news is that the ozone layer will eventually heal itself if we stop hurting it. However, there are still several nations that have not banned the use of CFCs. We also know now that there are more causes to global warming than just CFCs. Atmospheric chemists like Susan are continuing to work to convince the world to stop using these chemicals.

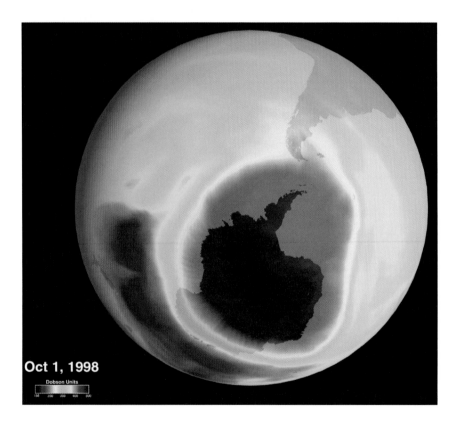

Oct 1, 1998

Dobson Units

Satellite instruments monitor the ozone layer, and scientists use their data to create images like this one from 1998, depicting the ozone hole over Anarctica. The blue and purple colors are where there is the least ozone, and the greens, yellows, and reds are where there is more ozone.

Find Out More

Chemical Heritage Foundation, "Mario Molina and Susan Solomon"
www.chemheritage.org/discover/online-resources/chemistry-in-history/
themes/public-and-environmental-health/environmental-chemistry/molina-and-
solomon.aspx

David, Laurie. *A Down-to-Earth Guide to Global Warming.* New York: Orchard Books,
2009.

Kaye, Cathryn Berger. *A Kid's Guide to Climate Change and Global Warming.* Min-
neapolis, Minn.: Free Spirit, 2009.

NOAA Celebrates 200 Years of Science, Service and Stewardship,
"Susan Solomon: Pioneering Atmospheric Scientist"
celebrating200years.noaa.gov/historymakers/solomon/welcome.html

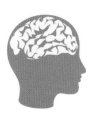

7

Dianne Gates-Anderson:
Protecting the Earth from Wastes

One of the unique things about environmental science is that it is constantly evolving. As more technology is developed, more problems arise from that technology. As an example, the amount of garbage we create is increasing. As the population increases and technology expands, more garbage is created. This waste causes pollution in the ground, water, and the air. It is a major problem that the Earth did not have until relatively recently. Environmental scientists must learn to identify these new problems—and then think up solutions for them. For Dianne Gates-Anderson, this is an exciting part of her job.

Waste

Waste is something that's discarded because it is no longer needed. You might refer to waste in your home as garbage. Waste can include paper, plastic, or food. Some waste does not harm the environment. This waste can break down and even help the environment. Decomposing food can fertilize plants and help them grow. Other types of waste, however, will harm the environment. This might be because they cannot be broken down or because they contain chemicals that are dangerous to plants, animals, and humans. Some harmful waste is created in factories, but you can find harmful waste right in your own home, such as old batteries and thermometers. This waste should never be thrown out in your household garbage. It must be disposed of in a special way.

When Dianne was a little girl, she never stopped asking questions. She found that science had the answers to a lot of her questions! Her passion for science didn't stop when she grew up. She earned her PhD in environmental engineering from the University of California at Berkeley. At the time, she was a single mother. Earning a PhD as a single parent is something Dianne still considers to be one of her greatest accomplishments.

After receiving a lot of specialized training, Dianne began to work at Lawrence Livermore National Laboratory in San Francisco, and she has been working there ever since. Her job is to find better ways to deal with waste management.

"I work to develop processes to treat these types of waste," Dianne says, "so they become less hazardous and help keep our community, families, and the environment safe."

To treat hazardous waste, scientists like Dianne use a combination of chemical and physical processes. They might use chemical processes like oxidation (what happens when you use bleach on dirty clothes) and neutralization (like mixing lemon juice or vinegar with baking soda) to treat **contaminated** solids

Today the U.S. government sets off nuclear bombs underground, in enormous pipes like these, so that scientists like Dianne can study the harmful effects of radiation without endangering the environment.

Preparing for the Worst

The nuclear bomb is a fairly new technology. It was first used on a large scale during World War II when two nuclear bombs were dropped on Japan. When it was used, few people understood the devastating effects it would have. Today we know that nuclear bombs are very powerful. They can kill a lot of people and make even more people sick with radiation poisoning. One of Dianne's tasks is helping us prepare for a possible nuclear explosion. How can we clean up the damage after it has been done? The radioactive waste would be very dangerous and hard to safely clean. In order to know the answers to these questions, scientists practice by detonating small bombs in a safe environment and seeing what the effects are. That way, we will know what to do if we ever need to deal with it in reality!

Dianne works at the Lawrence Livermore National Laboratory (LLNL), which is funded by the U.S. Department of Energy. The LLNL covers a square mile, and it contains some of the most powerful computers in the world.

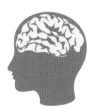

and liquids. The physical processes include absorption (like what happens when liquid is sucked into a sponge) and evaporation (what happens when you boil off a liquid). All these approaches, says Dianne, "can be combined with chemical processes or used by themselves to treat many of the different wastes that I encounter on my job."

Dianne's passion for learning is still going strong. She says, "I like the fact that because I am a **researcher** and an engineer, my job never becomes routine or boring because I get to move from one challenging problem to another, so there is always something new and interesting to look forward to."

Her advice to young students: "Take all of the math and science courses that you can. Don't see chemistry (or any science course for that matter) as being hard. Just think of it in terms of all the things around you that you can understand based on scientific principles."

Words to Know

Contaminated: polluted, impure.
Researcher: a person who investigates a question in search of an answer.

Find Out More

American Chemical Society, "Dianne D. Gates-Anderson"
portal.acs.org/portal/fileFetch/C/WPCP_006954/pdf/WPCP_006954.pdf

Morgan, Sally. *Household Waste*. North Mankato, Minn.: Smart Apple Media, 2008.

Silverman, Buffy. *Composting: Decomposition*. Mankato, Minn.: Heinneman-Raintree, 2008.

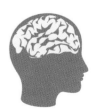

8

Stephanie Pfirman:

Studying Global Warming

Working with the environment can sometimes feel like solving a giant puzzle. You may notice a sudden change in the environment but not know what caused it. Scientists like Stephanie Pfirman notice these changes and do everything they can to find out why they are happening. Her area of expertise is arctic sea ice. She studies what gets caught in ice and tries to figure out how it got there.

Stephanie began her career at Colgate University, where she earned her bachelor's degree in 1978. In 1985, she earned her PhD in marine geology and geophysics from Massachusetts Institute of Technology (MIT). Since then, her specialty has become polar ice.

Environmental scientists like Stephanie can learn a great deal about our planet by studying the ice around the North Pole.

She spends a lot of her time educating others. One of her biggest projects was an exhibition on display at the American Museum of Natural History called "Global Warming: Understanding the Forecast." She has also served as a staff scientist for the U.S. House of Representatives Committee on Science.

Stephanie's main job is studying the ice found in the North Pole. The ice there is clouded and dirty, not clear and white as you might imagine. Scientists have discovered that pollution is what makes the polar ice dirty. Stephanie discovered that the ice is picking up pollution from warmer, more populated areas, and then releasing it when it eventually melts. The pollution can then harm the rest of the world.

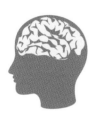

Problems in the Arctic

The arctic faces other troubles besides pollution in its ice. Many unique species of animals rely on the arctic ice to be their home. Every summer, some of the arctic ice melts. This is usually okay, because it freezes again during the colder months, but with global warming, more and more ice has been melting each summer. Scientists fear that if something is not done, all the ice will melt during the summer in a few decades. This could kill the species of animals that live there, including polar bears. Many environmental scientists are working hard to solve this complex problem.

Today, Stephanie Pfirman is doing her best to teach both children and adults about the ways pollution harms our world. She has worked at both Barnard College and Columbia University. One of her biggest concerns is obtaining funding for research. Scientists are interested and the public is concerned, but without research, little can be done. She hopes that more young people will get interested in the plight of the arctic ice and try to do something about it. Stephanie especially hopes that more women will become involved in science.

Find Out More

Archer, David. *Global Warming: Understanding the Forecast*. Hoboken, N.J.: John Wiley & Sons, 2012.

Barnard College, Columbia University, "Stephanie Pfirman"
www.barnard.edu/profiles/stephanie-pfirman

McKutcheon, Chuck. *What Are Global Warming and Climate Change: Answers for Young Readers*. Santa Fe: University of New Mexico Press, 2010.

Lena Ma: Cleaning the Environment with Ferns

9

Part of being an environmental scientist is figuring out what problems humans are causing. The other part is finding a way to fix these problems. Some scientists focus on finding the problems, while others focus on solving them. Lena Ma does both. She concentrates on fixing the problems within soil, but she also helps the world figure out where these problems are coming from.

Lena Ma began her education in China. In China, women only recently earned the right to pursue a career. Even so, women were not often given opportunities to become scientists. But Lena had made up her mind. She earned her bachelor's degree from the Shenyan Agricultural University, and then she moved to the United States, where she would have more opportunities.

After coming to the United States, Lena specialized in soil chemistry. She earned a master's degree in 1988 and a PhD in 1991 from Colorado State University. Today, Lena is a soil scientist.

Soil scientists study the soil. You might not realize how complex and interesting ordinary dirt can be! You also might not realize how important the soil is to our own lives. Plants absorb the nutrients they need from the soil. If the soil does not have these nutrients, or it has too many **foreign** chemicals, the plants may not be able to grow. Or they may soak up harmful chemicals. When animals or humans eat these plants, both the nutrients and the chemicals in the soil enter their bodies. Contaminated soil can reduce the amount of food humans have to eat—and it can allow harmful pollution to enter humans' bodies.

Lena specializes in metals within the soil. Lena also looks at water and waste to see where the metals come from in the first place. She studies how metals get into the soil and how the metals affect organisms. She also tries to find a way to safely remove the metals from the soil so that it is clean again.

In addition to her research, Lena works to educate others. She has written over 170 articles and is still publishing today. She has also helped raise an impressive $4 million for funding new research.

Lena has taught at two universities in the United States, Ohio State University and the University of Florida. In 2012, she began teaching at Nanjing University

A Natural Remedy

Human pollution causes a lot of problems. One harmful chemical that can be found in pollution is arsenic, which can harm plants and animals. Fortunately, some organisms have a way to cope with it. Lena's research group discovered a plant that can soak up arsenic, Chinese brake fern (Pteris vittata). Not only can it soak up a lot of arsenic, but it can do it very quickly. This suggests that this fern could be used to help reverse the effects of pollution in soil.

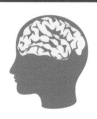

in China. As a female educator in China, she will hopefully inspire more young women there to follow in her footsteps.

As an environmental scientist, Lena has already done a lot for the planet—and she will continue to do still more!

Words to Know

Foreign: introduced from outside; not naturally belonging to.

Find Out More

Biogeochemistry & Environmental Remediation, "FACULTY: Lena Qiying Ma" hjxy.nju.edu.cn/maqy/product_view1.php?id=71

Chastain, Zachary. *Industrial Chemicals and Health*. Vestal, N.Y.: Village Earth Press, 2008.

10

Opportunities for Women in Environmental Science

Environmental science is a growing field. Because it is a relatively new form of scientific study, there is room for female students and scientists to enter this field with fewer barriers.

Environmental scientists held about 89,400 jobs in 2010. Most environmental scientists work for **private consulting firms** or for federal, state, or local governments. Environmental scientists usually work in offices and laboratories. They

Some environmental scientists even do their jobs in outer space! After she retired from NASA, Mae Jemison taught environmental studies at Dartmouth College, and she now works to teach younger children about the problems our planet faces.

58

also may spend time in the field gathering data and monitoring environmental conditions firsthand. Fieldwork can be physically demanding, and environmental scientists may work in all types of weather.

Some environmental scientists travel far away to do their work. If, for example, you want to study the hole in the ozone layer, like Susan Solomon, you may travel to Antarctica. Or if you want to study polar ice, you might set up camp on the other end of the planet, in the Arctic Circle, like Stephanie Pfirman. You might end up on remote islands in the Pacific Ocean that are being exposed to pollution. You might go to South America to study the rainforest.

Pay

The median annual wage of environmental scientists and specialists was $61,700 in 2011. (The median wage is the wage at which half the workers in an occupation earned more than that amount and half earned less.) The lowest 10 percent earned less than $37,850, and the top 10 percent earned more than $107,990.

Job Outlook

Employment of environmental scientists is expected to grow by 19 percent from 2010 to 2020, about as fast as the average for all other occupations. Increased public interest in protecting the Earth, as well as the increasing demands placed on the environment by population growth, is predicted to create a greater demand for environmental scientists. Further demand is also expected as a result of new and increasingly strict environmental laws and regulations.

Many, if not most, of the new jobs will be found in private consulting firms that help businesses **monitor** and manage environmental concerns and comply with regulations. For example, environmental consultants will help

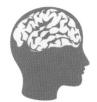

Environmental scientists have one of the most important jobs in the world: protecting our planet.

businesses develop practices that minimize waste, prevent pollution, and conserve resources. Other environmental scientists are expected to be needed to help urban planners develop and construct buildings, utilities, and transportation systems that protect natural resources and limit damage to the land.

Many job openings will also be created by scientists who retire, advance to management positions, or change careers. Environmental scientists often begin their careers as field analysts, research assistants, or technicians in laboratories and offices, but as they gain experience, they get more responsibilities. They may move into supervisory role, and eventually, they may be promoted to project leader, program manager, or some other management or research position. Other environmental scientists go on to work as researchers or faculty at colleges and universities.

Internationally, experts are more and more realizing the important roles women can play in protecting our planet. They have key roles to play in preserving the environment and natural resources, and in promoting sustainable development. Who knows? Passionate, intelligent, and committed female environmental scientists may be the ones who find the answers to serious problems like climate change and pollution!

Words to Know

Private consulting firms: companies hired by a person or organization to give advice on a specific problem.
Monitor: to watch closely.

Find Out More

California Polytechnic State University, "Career Services: What Can I Do with This Degree? Environmental Studies"
www.careerservices.calpoly.edu/content/student/wcid-envesci

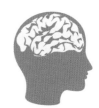

Cassio, Jim, and Alice Rush. *Green Careers: Choosing Work for a Sustainable Future.* Gabriola Island, B.C.: New Society, 2009.

Doyle, Kevin Lee., Sam Heizmann, Tanya Stubbs, and Bill Sharp. *The Complete Guide to Environmental Careers in the 21st Century.* Washington, D.C.: Island, 2009.

Flath, Camden. *Careers in Green Energy: Fueling the World with Renewable Resources.* Philadelphia, Penn.: Mason Crest, 2010.

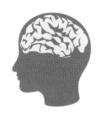

Index

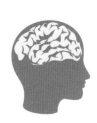

About the Author & Consultant

Shaina Indovino is a writer and illustrator living in Nesconset, New York. She graduated from Binghamton University, where she received degrees in sociology and English. She enjoyed the opportunity to apply both her areas of study to a topic that excites her: women in science. She hopes more young women will follow their calling toward what they truly love, whether it be science related or not.

Ann Lee-Karlon, PhD, is the President of the Association for Women in Science (AWIS) in 2014–2016. AWIS is a national non-profit organization dedicated to advancing women in science, technology, engineering, and mathematics. Dr. Lee-Karlon also serves as Senior Vice President at Genentech, a major biotechnology company focused on discovering and developing medicines for serious diseases such as cancer. Dr. Lee-Karlon holds a BS in Bioengineering from the University of California at Berkeley, an MBA from Stanford University, and a PhD in Bioengineering from the University of California at San Diego, where she was a National Science Foundation Graduate Research Fellow. She completed a postdoctoral fellowship at the University College London as an NSF International Research Fellow. Dr. Lee-Karlon holds several U.S. and international patents in vascular and tissue engineering.

Picture Credits

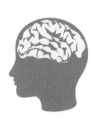